Chutneys, Pickles and Relishes

HOW THEY USED TO DO IT

Copyright © 2013 Two Magpies Publishing

An imprint of Read Publishing Ltd
Home Farm, 44 Evesham Road,
Cookhill, Alcester,
Warwickshire, B49 5LJ

Commissioning Editor Rose Hewlett
Written by Amelia Carruthers
Design by Zoë Horn Haywood

All Images remain the copyright property of their respective owners, all attributions and copyright licences are referenced at the rear of the book.

This book is copyright and may not be reproduced or copied in any way without the express permission of the publisher in writing.

British Library Cataloguing-in-Publication Data.
A catalogue record for this book is available from the British Library.

Contents

Introduction 3

Chutneys, Pickles and Relishes: A History 9

The Story of the Store Cupboard 15
   Staple Ingredients......................19

Sourcing Your Supplies 29

Equipment and Preparation 33
   Equipment Checklist 36

Measurements 37

Essential Skills............................43

Recipes 47
   Apple Chutney 50
   Piccalilli...............................54
   Sauerkraut.............................58
   Tomato Chutney........................62
   Caramelised Carrot and Orange Chutney 68
   English Herb Chutney 72
   Rhubarb and Date Chutney 76
   Roasted Lemon Chutney 80
   Pumpkin Chutney.......................84
   Pickled Cucumber and Dill 90
   Pickled Gherkins 95
   Lime Pickle............................98

Pickled Peppers........................102
Pickled Figs in Balsamic Vinegar..........106
Beetroot Relish..........................112
Chow Chow..............................116
Corn Relish.............................120
Red Pepper and Walnut Relish.............124
Gentleman's Relish......................128
Cranberry and Orange Relish..............134
Mediterranean Piccalilli..................138
Pickled Pears............................142
Sweet Chilli Chutney....................146
Marrow Chutney........................153
Pickled Nasturtiums.....................156
Pickled Onions..........................160
Radish Relish...........................164
Quince Chutney.........................168

Growing Guide!...........................172

Serving Suggestions........................175
  Have you thought about?.................177

Gorgeous Gifts............................179

'SOME BOOKS ARE TO BE TASTED, OTHERS TO BE SWALLOWED, AND SOME FEW TO BE CHEWED AND DIGESTED.'

Francis Bacon

Foreword

The simple pleasure of mastering practical household skills has been all but forgotten over the last century. We live in an overly convenient, disposable world in which things arrive pre-packed, ready-wrapped and lacking in any craft, care, or quality.

It's time to reject this attrition of what were once everyday skills, time to get back to basics, time to remember How They Used To Do It! The 'How They Used To Do It' series will take you back to the golden age of practical skills; an age where making and mending, cooking and preserving, brewing and bottling, were all done within the home. This fun, and proudly kitsch series will instruct you in a whole range of traditional skills that have fallen out of use, putting old knowledge into new hands. Using household items, nifty hints and tricks, and a little creativity you will be surprised what you can achieve.

The series has been carefully curated from a wealth of original resources to provide a wonderful blend of social history and practical instruction. The knowledge within these pages has been sourced from rare books, old newspapers and forgotten magazines to inform a whole new generation about How They Used To Do It .

Introduction

Introduction

WELCOME TO THE WONDERFUL WORLD OF CHUTNEYS, PICKLES AND RELISHES.

Introduction

The main benefit of homemade produce is that *you* can pick the best and purest ingredients yourself. In an increasingly synthetic age, knowing exactly what has gone into your lovingly created products is a rare luxury. With just a little time, effort and outlay, the end result is incredibly rewarding!

Herein lies the philosophy behind the 'How They Used To Do It' series. With this little book in your hands you can turn a humble kitchen into a hub of activity, happily passing many a rainy (or sunny!) day creating delicious and refreshing concoctions. As well as lots of classic recipes, this book is filled with tips and techniques on making the perfect preserve. What's more, you don't even need lots of equipment or a vast array of ingredients to get started.

Making your own chutneys, pickles and relishes at home is very often cheaper than buying them - perfect for the

Introduction

thrifty home-chef. The cost of ingredients is low (especially if you pick them yourself), and by creating large batches, you can save a huge amount of money. It is *incredibly* easy to make chutneys, pickles and relishes at home… Preserving vegetables by turning them into chutney, for example, involves cooking (to reduce the vegetables moisture content and to kill bacteria, yeasts, etc.), flavouring, the addition of vinegar, and sealing within an airtight jar (to prevent recontamination). Thats it! Pickles and relishes are largely similar, but generally involve the addition of vinegar and other spices to often uncooked (or partially cooked) vegetables, producing a slightly 'chunkier' result.

The wonderful thing about making your own homemade products is the fun one can have with creating customised labels and garnishes to the finished jars (think finely chopped veg, citrus zest, herb sprigs) – a perfect vintage-

Introduction

inspired present as well as personal treat. We hope that the reader is inspired by this book to start making their own chutneys, pickles and relishes; a delicious, historical, as well as rewarding pastime. Enjoy.

Amelia Carruthers

Introduction

"Perhaps Ruskin is no longer fashionable, but sometimes I like to remind myself of one thing he wrote concerning cooking. 'Cookery means the knowledge of Medea and of Circe and of Helen and of the Queen of Sheba. It means the knowledge of all herbs and fruits and balms and spices, and all that is healing and sweet in the fields and groves, and savoury in meats. It means carefulness and inventiveness and readiness of appliances. It means the economy of your grandmothers, and the science of the modern chemist; it means much testing and no wasting; it means English thoroughness and French Art and Arabian hospitality; and, in fine, it means that you are to be perfectly and always ladies… loaf givers."

Mollie Stanley Wrench,
The Complete Illustrated Cookery *(1935)*

Chutneys, Pickles and Relishes: A History

Chutneys, Pickles and Relishes: A History

For time immemorial, fruit and vegetables have been regarded not merely as an article of food, but also as a luxury. The season during which each ripe produce could be obtained was in most cases of only short duration, and ripe fruit and vegetables were exceedingly perishable. Hence, some method of preservation was a matter of importance, and one of the most convenient processes consisted of adding vinegar in some form or another, the resultant product being known as chutneys, pickles and relishes!

Pickling is the process of preserving food by anaerobic fermentation, in brine or vinegar; resulting in perishable foods being available for months longer than they would otherwise. If the food contains sufficient moisture, a pickling brine may be produced simply by adding dry salt. For example, German sauerkraut and Korean kimchi are produced by salting the vegetables to draw out excess water. Chutney on

Chutneys, Pickles and Relishes: A History

the other hand, can be either wet or dry, and have a coarse or fine texture - some sweetened, and some sour. It usually contains a mixture of spices, vegetables and/or fruits. Vinegar and lemon juice are often added as natural preservatives, and occasionally fermentation in the presence of salt may be used to create acid. There is very little difference between a chutney and a relish in the English language. Both are added to meals to give flavour, and many would argue that relish is in fact a form of chutney. It differs from the ubiquitous chutney though, in that a *relish* will generally consist of *discernible* vegetable or fruit pieces in a sauce. Chutneys are most usually cooked to a reduction, thereby making a more 'jam' like consistency.

Pickling began 4000 years ago, using cucumbers native to India; the resultant product known as 'achar.' The technique was also used by the Romans, who made a concentrated fish

Chutneys, Pickles and Relishes: A History

pickle called 'garum.' Although these products arose out of necessity, people enjoyed the resultant flavours too! Early chutneys were reasonably similar in preparation and usage to a pickle, and they date back as far as 500 BC. Although also famous as an Indian dish, this method of preserving food actually originated in Northern Europe and was adopted by the British empire, who then started exporting food to the colonies including Australia and America. However, the combination of greater and more varied imports to Britain, as well as new abilities to refrigerate food, meant that chutneys fell out of favour and were relegated to military and colonial use. The British Royal Navy particularly utilised lime pickle/chutney to ward off scurvy on journeys to the new world. Consequently, it was around this time (about 1780) that chutney appeared as a popular appetizer dish in India.

Chutneys, Pickles and Relishes: A History

The history of chutneys, pickles and relishes is thus inextricably tied with the history of exploitation and colonisation. British rule over the Indian subcontinent relied on preserved foodstuffs such as lime pickles, chutneys and marmalades. It was only in the nineteenth century that types of chutney such as 'Major Grey's' or 'Bengal Club', specifically created for western tastes, were shipped back to Europe. The tradition of chutney, pickle and relish making then spread quickly through the English-speaking world, especially in the Caribbean and American South, where

Chutneys, Pickles and Relishes: A History

chutney is still a popular condiment for ham, pork, and fish. Relishes are particularly fashionable in America, with pickled cucumber the most widely available condiment. An especially notable relish is *Gentleman's Relish*, invented in 1828 by Ben Elvin, which contains spiced Anchovy. It is traditionally spread sparingly atop unsalted butter on toast. Amusingly, Worcester sauce was discovered from a forgotten barrel of special relish in the London basement of the *Lea and Perrins* Chemist shop!

As is evident, the story of food preservation, and specifically the modern usages of chutneys, pickles and relishes encompasses far more than just culinary history. Ancient civilisations, colonisation and accidental discoveries all played their part in creating these staples of our modern diet.

The Story of the Store Cupboard

The Story of the Store Cupboard

"A STORE-CUPBOARD, FROM WHICH ONE CAN PRODUCE POTS OF HOMEMADE PRESERVE, IS A GREAT ADVANTAGE..."

Mollie Stanley Wrench (1935)

The Story of the Store Cupboard

Kitchens have come an awfully long way in the past century, as have the supplies stocked in pantries and larders. Before modern conveniences such as fridges and freezers, one of the biggest hurdles housewives had to overcome was the task of preserving, and it was no mean feat! It is hard to imagine a world without the convenience of modern kitchen appliances, and keeping food fresh was a daily challenge. There are many simple preservation methods that can be carried out in the kitchen, without the use of modern conveniences. Salt can be used to cure meat and fish, and pickles with vinegar can preserve vegetables. The drying of fruit, herbs and spices is especially useful, and can be used across a wide range of recipes including sweets. Luckily, alongside pickling, chutneys and relishes were also perfect for preserving these much needed foodstuffs!

The Story of the Store Cupboard

Having a well-stocked larder was the mark of a good housewife, and before easy preservation and storage methods became commonplace, homemade chutneys, pickles and relishes were de-rigueur. Lessening food waste is a thoroughly worthwhile project, both then and now.

During the summer months especially, when certain vegetables (and fruits!) are in abundance, making batches of chutneys and relishes to store is a great way of ensuring none of the delicious produce is wasted. Although the pickle and chutney-makers of the past would not have had this option, your homemade goodies can be stored in the fridge (or freezer) for many months, allowing you to enjoy your hard work throughout the winter.

The Story of the Store Cupboard

STAPLE INGREDIENTS

When making chutneys, pickles and relishes, thankfully - there aren't many. All you will need are vinegar, spices and sugar, possibly salt, herbs or citrus and the 'main ingredient' for your chutney, pickle or relish.

Vinegar, Spices and Sugar are the three most important, and consistently necessitated ingredients, so it is worthwhile taking a little time getting to know them….

The Story of the Store Cupboard

Vinegar

"If you pour oil and vinegar into the same vessel, you would call them not friends but opponents."

Aeschylus (525-456 BC)

Vinegar is a liquid consisting mainly of 'acetic acid' and water. The acid is produced by the fermentation of ethanol by acetic acid bacteria. Today, vinegar is mainly used as a cooking ingredient, but historically, as the most easily available mild acid, it had a great variety of industrial, medicinal and domestic uses. Some of which (such as a general household cleanser) are still promoted today!

The Story of the Store Cupboard

This is what the How They Used To Do It series is all about, not letting anything go to waste, and discovering traditional wisdom on modern issues.

There are so many different types of vinegar, including apple cider, balsamic, date, honey, malt, rice, sherry, wine, distilled white versions… the list goes on. It was first discovered in ancient civilisations when grape juice was accidentally left - and turned into wine. Wine in turn, if also left undisturbed, turned into vinegar. Whilst this was not such a welcome transformation, over time, the multitudinous uses of vinegar were discovered. Helen of Troy apparently bathed in vinegar to relax, whilst Cleopatra demonstrated its powers of solvency by dissolving pearls in the liquid to win a bet that she could consume a fortune.

The Story of the Store Cupboard

Today, vinegar is commonly used in food preparation, in particular the pickling processes, vinaigrettes and other salad dressings. It is also an ingredient in sauces such as mustard, ketchup and mayonnaise. It is also, as we have already discovered, sometimes used when making chutneys and other condiments. Its preservative qualities mean that vinegar can last indefinitely without the use of refrigeration – a truly useful foodstuff both then and now!

Spices

A spice is a dried seed, fruit, root, bark or vegetable substance primarily used for flavouring, colouring or preserving food. Spices are distinguished from herbs, which are parts of leafy green plants also used for flavouring or as garnishes. The spice trade developed throughout South Asia and Middle East in around 2000 BCE with cinnamon and pepper, and in East Asia with herbs and pepper. The Egyptians used many varied herbs for embalming and their demand for exotic herbs helped stimulate world trade.

Spices were among the most sought after and expensive products available in Europe in the Middle Ages, the most common being black pepper, cinnamon (and the cheaper alternative cassia), cumin, nutmeg, ginger and cloves. Given medieval medicine's main theory of humorism, spices and herbs were indispensable to balance 'humors' in food, a daily basis for good health at a time of recurrent pandemics.

With the discovery of the New World came new spices, including allspice, bell and chili peppers, vanilla, and chocolate. This kept the spice trade profitable, with America as a late comer with its new seasonings, well into the nineteenth century and the present day. In times of austerity, especially during the two world wars, the enterprising housewife utilised spices to great extent; especially in the form of pickles and relishes to liven up home-grown fruit and vegetables. Spices are such an intriguing ingredient, with a cross-cultural history all of their own, affecting economics, politics and culinary endeavours. They are as much appreciated today as they were in the past, so happy spicing!

The Story of the Store Cupboard

Sugar

*"These high wild hills and rough uneven ways
Draw out our miles and make them wearisome
But yet your fair discourse hath been as sugar
Making the hard way sweet and delectable"*

William Shakespeare, Richard II *(1595)*

These days, sugar is a staple ingredient - found in almost all pantries across the country. It is readily available in many different forms; granulated, caster, demerara, muscovado... etc. But go back one hundred, or even fifty years though, and this most certainly would not have been the case. Before the seventeenth century, in Britain and throughout most of Europe, honey was the main ingredient used to sweeten

The Story of the Store Cupboard

foods. But after Britain took Jamaica and other parts of the West Indies from Spain in 1655, this changed. By 1750 there were 120 British refining factories, producing 30,000 tonnes of sugar a year from sugar cane. Sugar was heavily taxed though and it was not until 1874 that this levy was removed and sugar became more affordable.

Until the late nineteenth century, sugar came in the form of 'sugarloaf' which was essentially a hard block of the raw material. Housewives would buy their sugar in tall, conical loaves, and trim off what they needed with special iron sugar-cutters called sugar nips. If a recipe called for fine, granulated sugar, then a little elbow grease and a pestle and mortar would be enthusiastically employed! Whilst granulated sugar was not far behind, the two World Wars put the brakes on the nation's sugar consumption. It was among the first items to be rationed in 1918, alongside butter, margarine, lard and

The Story of the Store Cupboard

meat. During the 1930s, the country's love affair with sugar came under attack. As World War II air raid sirens sounded throughout Britain's cities, a different war was being fought behind closed doors. Trade routes to the UK were targeted during the war, and food supplies quickly dwindled. On 8th January 1940, bacon, butter and sugar were rationed by the government, followed in subsequent months by meat, tea, jam and much more.

Despite being armed with her government-issued ration book, the average housewife's weekly shopping basket was suddenly much lighter than before. Creating tasty and nutritious meals for the family became a real challenge for many. Sugar became a very precious resource, and a thriving black market quickly sprung up as a result of the strict rationing. With legitimate supplies so very low, mothers had

The Story of the Store Cupboard

to be increasingly inventive in order to supply their children and husbands with sweet treats. To give you a picture of 'how they used to do it' in the 1940s - The average allowance of sugar was 8 oz (227g) a week.

Sourcing Your Supplies

Sourcing Your Supplies

These days, we are incredibly lucky to be sure of a well stocked pantry. Without the convenience of large supermarkets, it could take a busy housewife the best part of the day to fill her shopping basket with supplies for the week from her local high street.

Making your own chutneys, pickles and relishes is a fantastic way to use up surplus produce, much of which you may have grown yourself, or naturally foraged. Work out when the vegetables or fruits are in abundance, what time of year is best to pick them, and most importantly, where you can find them. In april, the first cabbages might make an appearance, followed in the mid summer months by all range of treats; tomatoes, radishes, onions and nasturtiums... As we move into autumn, delicious

Sourcing Your Supplies

veggies such as beetroots and quinces will follow on. For the more exotic chutney or relish though, as well as for necessary ingredients such as lemons or limes, your local food-store should have everything you need.

Finding the best ingredients before you put your apron on and start cooking is important, as the lovelier your initial ingredients are, the lovelier the end-result will be. Look at the local produce on offer in your area. It is so often the case that the best things to eat are the things that grow locally, are in season, and haven't travelled a huge distance. Not only do such items taste better than their imported counterparts, but it is far kinder to the environment to use what is nearby. Perhaps you have a wonderful local greengrocer who can supply you with seasonal vegetables, or a brilliant local health food shop where you can stock up on herbs and spices? Use your local suppliers and their expertise, as their knowledge will be rather useful to you while you are still getting to grips with the basics.

Sourcing Your Supplies

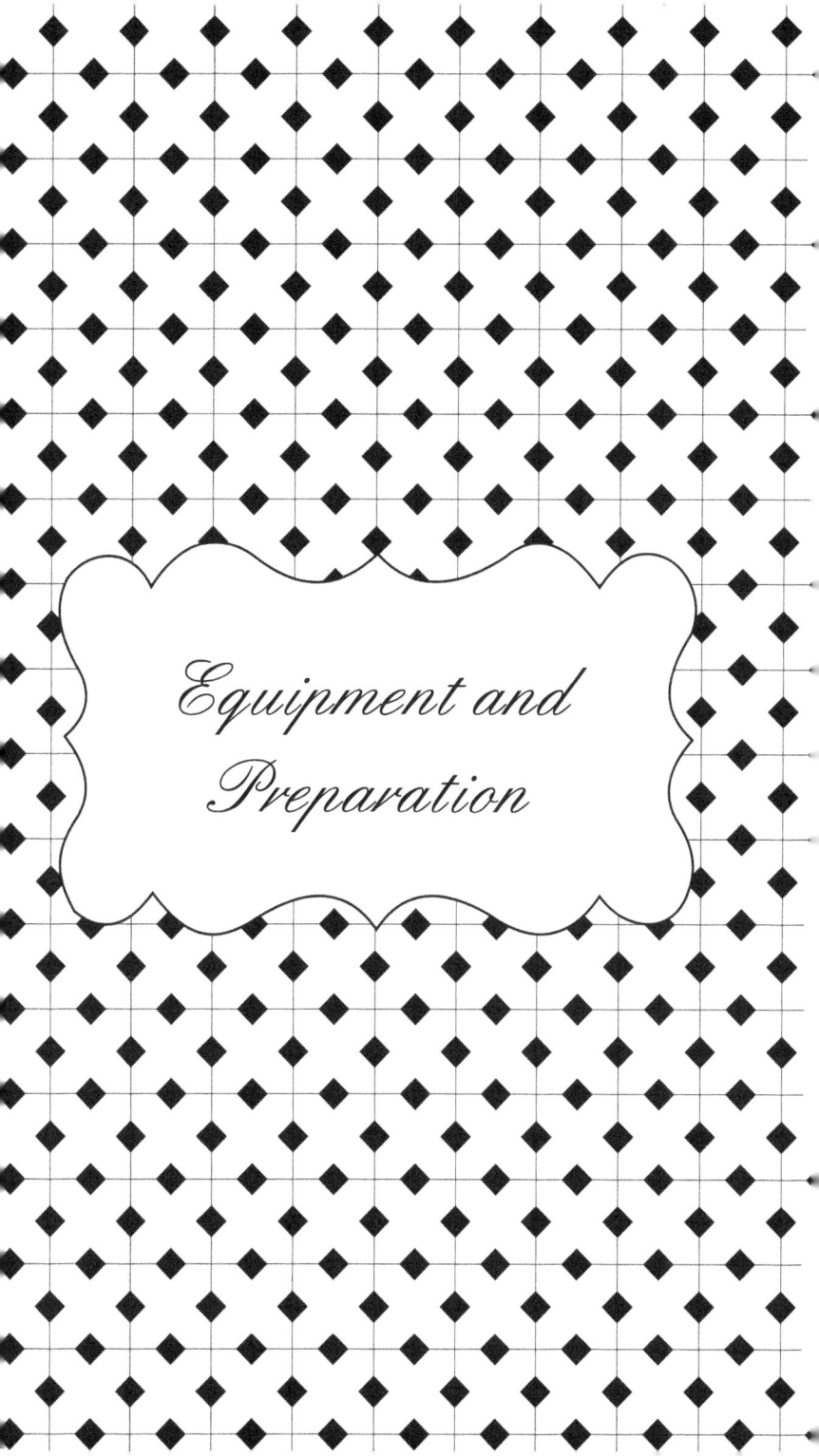

Equipment and Preparation

Equipment and Preparation

Thankfully, for small-scale home cooking, you will need very little specialist equipment. The list of utensils and equipment is not huge, but it is important you have the basics at your fingertips. Your kitchen utensils are the tools of your trade, as it were, and you'll get the best results from your chutney, pickle or relish making if you take the time to source the right ones.

The equipment needed is rather basic, and you may already have most of it around the house. You will need saucepans (heavy-bottomed jam boilers work best), any earthenware or non-porous bowls and plenty of glass jars (for storage; size and amount dependent on the batch size you are intending), as well as occasionally a sieve for straining. Wax paper discs to seal the jars will protect the lids against the vinegars acidic properties. Sharp knives are also invaluable, and will save you a lot of time and effort! Wooden spoons are great for stirring at high temperatures (as they do not conduct heat), and metal spoons are better for skimming off any unwanted pieces which may rise to the surface.

Equipment and Preparation

Always ensure the fruits or vegetables have been washed thoroughly, especially if they have been gathered from low plants, or trees that are near roads.

The recipes in this book will use either 500g or 1kg of vegetables (if this is the main ingredient), which should produce between three and six traditional jam jars, or the equivalent of pickle. These amounts are only a rough guide though, and it is always better to overestimate the amount of jars you many need! The amount of chutney or relish you produce will depend on how strong you wish the end result to be though. Some people prefer much thicker, viscous products, whilst others will only be looking for a 'chunky mix.' Have fun experimenting and just use what you've got!

Equipment and Preparation

EQUIPMENT CHECKLIST

SAUCEPAN
(preferably heavy-bottomed)

*

BOWLS
(for storing the fruit or vegetables)

*

LARGE SPOONS
(wooden are the most useful)

*

SHARP KNIVES
(for finely chopping the vegetables!)

*

GLASS JARS
(for storage and presentation)

*

WAXED DISCS
(to protect your jam jars' lids)

Measurements

Measurements

*"Haste still pays haste, and leisure answers leisure;
Like doth quit like, and Measure still for Measure."*

William Shakespeare, Measure for Measure *(1604)*

Here, we were in a dilemma...

Of course, in the 'golden-age' of home cooking, measurements would have been very rough; using simple ratios was the most common practice. i.e. 'two parts vinegar to one part sugar' and so on. Others would have utilised kitchen cups (which, pre-1890s could have been any size!), and yet other chutney and pickle makers, as we move into the twentieth century, would have started using ounces, pounds and pints. Cups have been used in cookery for generations, their use gained in popularity after an American culinary expert called Fanny Farmer introduced them as a standardised form of

Measurements

measurement in recipes. Her emphasis on accuracy and consistency in recipes was groundbreaking for the time, and has since sparked a revolution in the way we cook. Fanny published her best-known cookery book 'The Boston Cooking-School Cook Book' in 1896, in which she stressed the importance of levelling off the cup as you measure. This may seem insignificant, but before her clever intervention, cooks had to make do with instructions such as 'a large dash', 'a goodly pinch', and even 'butter the size of an egg'. Rather amusing, but a little inconsistent, don't you agree?

We are aware that most of our readers will not possess standardised 'chefs cups', and nor may they be au-fait with the exact quantities of a 'goodly pinch.' For this reason, we

Measurements

decided to update all the old recipes into grams; leaving the traditional ingredients and methods - but just making life a little easier for the modern cook.

If you do wish for complete historical accuracy, we have included a handy table for converting grams to ounces to cups, and likewise cups to pints to milliliters. Whether you prefer to don the traditional cup, frilly pinafore and wooden spoon, or take a more updated approach to the classics - we leave the choice up to you…

Measurements

Cups to Classics' - Conversion Chart

Water	1 Cup	8 Fluid oz	½ Pint	237 ml
Sugar	1 Cup	4.5 oz	n/a	200g
	1 Tablespoon	0.89 oz	n/a	12g

To summarise...

1 cup = 4.5 ounces
1 ounce = 28.34 grams
1 pound = 0.453 kilograms
1 gram = 0.035 ounces
1 kilogram = 2.2 pounds
1 Fluid oz = 29.57 milliliters.

Measurements

More handy weight conversions:

1 Tablespoon = 5 Fluid oz, or 14.79 ml
3 Teaspoons = 1 Tablespoon
4 Tablespoons = ¼ Cup
16 Tablespoons = 1 Cup

Essential Skills

Essential Skills

There really is only one really essential 'skill' that the would-be chutney, pickle or relish maker will have to master, and that is: Sterilisation. This technique though, is done in exactly the same way, using exactly the same methods as it always has been. Some things just can't be improved upon!

Sterilisation

It is very important that you use sterilised jars to store your jam or jelly in, both during preparation and in the later stages of the process when you are storing your creations. This will help them to keep for longer, as it will remove any bacteria, yeasts or fungi and protect your liquids. Jars and that have not been sterilised properly will infect the food inside, meaning it will spoil very quickly and need to be thrown away. Sterilisation is a very simple process though, and can

Essential Skills

be done in a number of ways. The simplest way to sterilise your equipment at home is to wash the bottles or jars in very hot soapy water, rinse in more very hot water, and place them into an oven on the lowest setting (275°F/130°C/Gas 1) for twenty minutes. Ensure you use the bottles when they are still warm, and also that they are airtight when sealed to prevent bacteria entering the bottle.

N.B: Do not put cold liquids into hot jars, or hot liquids into cold jars; this may result in the glass shattering; a messy and dangerous problem to fix!

Essential Skills

"The housewife need not be afraid of her preserves spoiling if she follows the few simple directions given here… Complete sterilisation of the glasses and jars, and also the utensils used is necessary if your fruit is to keep perfectly. This is done by immersing the glasses and jars in hot water, or better still, placing them in cold water in a vessel and bringing the water to the boiling point. A little baking soda added to the water will aid in this sterilisation. Keep the glasses and jars filled with boiling water or immersed in boiling water until you are ready to fill them. Don't forget that what is necessary for the jars is also necessary for the lids!"

Mary M. Wright, Preserving and Pickling *(1917)*

Traditional Favourites

Every housekeeper knows what a comfort it is to have a good supply of her own preserves which she can rely upon when the winter season comes around…. It is surprising how quickly the pantry shelves may be filled with these delicacies by doing up a small quantity at a time, and the expense is scarcely felt at all.

APPLE CHUTNEY

Traditional folklore is brimming with references to the apple tree's virtues. This ancient, and thoroughly English tree has provided abundant food for centuries, and has many uses in the kitchen (both sweet and savoury) as well as in herbal remedies. The crab apple (Pyrus Malus) is native to Britain, and is the wild ancestor of all our modern-day cultivated varieties. In 1931, when writing Modern Herbal, a Mrs Grieve stated that there used to be 2,000 varieties of apple, but with the unfortunate decline of private orchards, many of these wonderful fruits have been lost. This is a true classic and a great starter recipe, so delicious and so easy to make - perfect with pork and crackling.

Apple Chutney

If they are in season (early autumn), and you happen to have a tree nearby, why not try replacing the apples with crab apples? A spiced crab apple chutney (think turmeric, ginger and chilli) would be a lovely accompaniment to a warming winter roast. It would also be wonderful with cold meats or added to a traditional gravy - giving a hint of fruit sweetness to your dishes.

Apple Chutney

1kg cooking apples

600g sugar (muscovado or demerara works best)

600ml cider vinegar

300g raisins

2 shallots (regular onions would work just as well)

2 tablespoons of whole-grain mustard

3cm (roughly) of ginger, grated

A pinch of salt

Apple Chutney

1. Core, peel (optional) and roughly chop the apples. **2.** Place the apples, along with all the other ingredients into a large, heavy-bottomed saucepan. **3.** Bring the temperature up, and cook the ingredients on a medium boil for a couple of minutes. **4.** Then, allow to simmer for roughly thirty minutes. Cook until the mixture has obtained a thick, 'jam' like consistency. **5.** If sufficiently cooked, remove from the heat and allow to cool slightly. **6.** Transfer your warm chutney into warm sterilised jars. Cover with a wax paper disc and seal.

PICCALILLI

"Cauliflower is nothing but cabbage with a college education."

Mark Twain (1835-1910)

Piccalilli is an English interpretation of a classic Indian pickle; a relish of chopped pickled vegetables (most usually cauliflower and marrow) and spices. The Oxford English Dictionary traces the word to the middle of the eighteenth century when, in 1758, Hannah Glasse described how 'to make Paco-Lilla, or Indian Pickle.' Our modern recipes, and the one listed here - are all derivations from this original

Piccalilli

dish. The current spelling of 'piccalilli' only appeared in 1799, in an advertisement placed in The Times.

Traditional British piccalilli tends to contain mustard and turmeric, and is used as a tangy accompaniment to dishes including cold meats, cheeses and tomatoes. A Ploughman's Lunch being the true How They Used To Do It classic. Today, piccalilli is produced both commercially and domestically, the latter product being a mainstay of Women's Institute and farmhouse stalls; delicious as well as cheap to produce. A perfect start for the home-relisher! Here, personal adaptations and experimentation is key, so use whatever vegetables you have to hand…

Piccalilli

*Vegetables to make up 1kg
(of roughly equal amounts). Try…*

Cauliflower Florets

Cucumber

French Beans

Garden Marrow

Pickled Onions

Spices:

1 tablespoon whole-grain mustard

1 teaspoon ginger (ground or more grated)

1 teaspoon turmeric

1 large clove of garlic

500ml white malt vinegar

100g sugar
(again, demerara or muscovado work best)

2 tablespoons cornflour

Salt (to taste)

Piccalilli

1. Place the vegetables and salt in a glass or ceramic bowl. Leaving the vegetables and the salt overnight will result in crisper pickles, as the salt helps to pull the moisture out of the vegetables and makes them crisper. **2.** The next morning, discard the liquid, rinse and dry the vegetables. **3.** Place the vinegar and spices into a large, heavy-bottomed saucepan and bring to the boil. **4.** Add the vegetables to the vinegar and bring down to a simmer. Cook on a very low temperature for about twenty minutes, or until the vegetables are tender. **5.** Add the sugar and cornflour to the mix, stirring constantly. It should start to thicken. **6.** If sufficiently cooked, remove the piccalilli from the heat and allow to cool slightly. **7.** Put the warm mix into warm, sterilised jars. Cover with a wax paper disc and seal. Store for at least three weeks before opening!

SAUERKRAUT

"Cabbage, although often ill-treated by the way in which it is cooked, has medicinal values, of which the ancients wrote, and a cup of water in which cabbage is cooked is supposed to be health giving if drunk slowly. Given a preliminary blanching, cooked cabbage can be made to eat more delicate. Cooked in milk till tender it is supposed to be much more digestible, To prevent the smell of cabbage from escaping and scenting the house disagreeably, tie a crust of baked bread in muslin and lay this in the saucepan when cooking."

Ethelind Fearnon,
Jams, Jellies and Preserves – How to Make them *(1956)*

Sauerkraut

Sauerkraut, directly translated as 'sour cabbage' is finely cut cabbage that has been fermented. This gives it a longer shelf-life and a distinctive sour flavour, wonderful as a condiment on various meats and sandwiches. Although famed as a traditional German dish, pickled cabbage is mentioned by the Roman writer Cato (in his De Agri Cultura) and Columella (in his De re Rustica). It is believed to have been re-introduced to Europe around 1,000 years later by Genghis Kahn. Such dishes provided much needed nutrients to the British population in times of hardship, especially during winter. In fact, the British explorer James Cook always took a store of sauerkraut on his sea voyages, since experience had taught him it prevented scurvy. If it was good enough for an intrepid explorer, its good enough for this How They Used To Do It!

Sauerkraut

**1 green cabbage
(red cabbage works just as well though)**

1 ½ tablespoons salt

**1 tablespoon caraway seeds
(optional flavouring)**

Sauerkraut

1. Sauerkraut needs so few ingredients, because when combined with the salt, the cabbage releases its own juices, forming a natural brine. **2.** Discard the outer leaves of the cabbage, and very finely slice the rest of it (avoiding the core). **3.** Transfer the cabbage, with the salt to a large glass or ceramic bowl, and mix in the salt, combining with your hands until is has turned limp and slightly watery. **4.** Pack the cabbage into jars (larger kilner clip tops work best). Make sure to pour any remaining liquid over the cabbage in the jar. **5.** Weigh the cabbage down with something flat and heavy, then cover the jar with some cloth and rubber bands. If it needs extra liquid to keep it fully submerged, add a little salt and water solution. **6.** Place the jar in a cool, dark place and allow it to ferment for about ten days. Taste as you go though, and if it tastes good, seal the jar and place in the refrigerator. **7.** How long the sauerkraut ferments for is completely up to you, it should keep for at least four months when sealed and refrigerated though.

Tomato Chutney

TOMATO CHUTNEY

Tomatoes were not grown in England until the 1590s, and one of the earliest cultivators was John Gerard, a barber-surgeon. He published a book, Herbal in 1597 which was largely plagiarized from continental sources - but was one of the earliest discussions of the tomato in England. He believed it was poisonous though, and in fact the raw fruit does have low levels of tomatine (found in the stalks) but is not dangerous. Gerard's views were highly influential, and the tomato was not considered for eating until the late seventeenth century! By the mid eighteenth century however, tomatoes were widely eaten in Britain as soups,

Tomato Chutney

broths and as a garnish. By the mid nineteenth century were described 'to be seen in great abundance in all our vegetable markets.'

This classic chutney is very simple to make, and perfect with a thick slice of traditional English cheddar and bread, or even with a burger or vegetable curry. It is versatile and not too sweet, perfect for preserving a summer glut of this lovely vegetable. A juicy and spicy concoction, unripe green tomatoes can even be used too - great for using up a great little fruit which would otherwise go to waste!

Tomato Chutney

1kg tomatoes

500g red onions

Spices:

3 large garlic cloves

1 small chilli

3cm ginger

½ tablespoon paprika

250g sugar (demerara or muscovado)

150ml wine vinegar

Tomato Chutney

1. Chop the tomatoes, chilli, garlic and ginger, and finely slice the onions. **2.** Place all the ingredients into a large, heavy-bottomed saucepan. **3.** Bring the temperature up, and cook the ingredients on a medium boil for a couple of minutes. **4.** Then, allow to simmer for roughly forty-five minutes. Cook until the mixture has obtained a thick, 'jam' like consistency. **5.** If sufficiently cooked, remove from the heat and allow to cool slightly. **6.** Transfer your warm chutney into warm sterilised jars. Cover with a wax paper disc and seal.

Choice Chutneys

"For now, not one, nor two,
But every maid I view
I love, with love that widens with my years.
And when I pass away,
Reader, weep not, but say,
Chutney is with the cherubs - pretty dears!"

Robert C. Caldwell, The Chutney Lyrics *(1871)*

CARAMELISED CARROT AND ORANGE CHUTNEY

The wild ancestors of the carrot are likely to have come from Iran and Afghanistan, but over time and with selective breeding, they have become sweeter and less 'woody' - producing the familiar garden vegetable we see today. In early use, carrots were grown for their aromatic leaves and seeds, not their roots. They appear to have been introduced to Europe via Spain by the Moors in the eighth century though, in both red and yellow colours. Our modern orange-coloured carrots first appeared in the Netherlands (whose flag contained orange) in the seventeenth century. They came to England soon after, where they were quickly adopted and

Caramelised Carrot and Orange Chutney

grown by the populace. Fittingly for this How They Used To Do It, carrots were a favourite of wartime Britain, bringing much needed vitamin A to the population. Rather amusingly, the government responded to a temporary oversupply of this vegetable by suggesting that the RAF's night flying successes were due to heightened vision caused by 'carotene.' The ruse worked though, and consumption of carrots increased sharpy!

This lovely, sweet and warming chutney is great with honey and mustard, and would be an intriguing addition to a spinach or apple dish. If you add some spicing (chilli and ginger would work well), this chutney would also be fantastic with curry.

Caramelised Carrot and Orange Chutney

1kg carrots (approximately 15)

2 small onions

1 orange (juiced and zested)

150g soft, dark sugar

450ml white wine vinegar

A dash of oil

Caramelised Carrot and Orange Chutney

1. Grate the carrots, and place them in a large, heavy-bottomed pan with a little olive oil to prevent them sticking. Also add the onions, finely sliced and the zest from the orange. **2.** Cook on a low heat until the carrots are soft. Then add the sugar and cook over a medium heat until the sugar has nicely caramelised. **3.** Pour over the vinegar and orange juice and bring the whole mixture to the boil. Continue to cook until all the liquid has evaporated and the chutney has a thick consistency. **4.** Take the mixture off the heat and allow to cool slightly. **5.** Place the warm chutney into warm, sterilised jars. Cover with a wax paper disc and seal. Leave for at least a week before opening.

ENGLISH HERB CHUTNEY

Here, anything goes! The brilliant thing about making savoury herb chutneys, is that you are in complete control of what you add into them. Once you have mastered the basic technique, you are in charge of the variations. Many herbs make great companions; rosemary and garlic with mint or parsley; fennel and marjoram with lemon thyme; or basil and sage with tarragon. You should be aiming for is a sweet yet piquant chutney though - so think about the herbs you would like to see as accompaniments to your regular dishes.

English Herb Chutney

We particularly recommend this version of a classically English apple chutney, flavoured with aromatic but subtle thyme and rosemary. The hint of lemon and garlic ensures a sophisticated finish and it is useful for livening stews, soups and gravies. If you like, try replacing the apple with pear. This combination would be a lovely accompaniment to soft blue cheeses.

English Herb Chutney

500g cooking apples (or pears)
150g soft, dark sugar
300ml cider vinegar
1 sprig of thyme (finely chopped leaves)
1 sprig of rosemary (finely chopped leaves)
1 lemon (zested)
1 clove of garlic

English Herb Chutney

---

1. Core, peel and roughly chop the apples. **2.** Place the apples into a large, heavy-bottomed saucepan. Add the chopped thyme, rosemary, garlic and the lemon zest. **3.** Bring the temperature up, and cook the ingredients on a medium boil for a couple of minutes. **4.** Then, allow to simmer for roughly thirty minutes. Or until the apples (or pears) are nice and soft. The mixture should obtain a thick, 'jam' like consistency. **5.** If sufficiently cooked, remove from the heat and allow to cool slightly. **6.** Transfer your warm herb chutney into warm sterilised jars. Cover with a wax paper disc and seal.

RHUBARB AND DATE CHUTNEY

"It is only the modern that ever becomes old-fashioned."

Oscar Wilde (1854-1900)

A marriage of east and west!

It is difficult to think of a more traditional English ingredient than Rhubarb - the main ingredient of wonderful crumbles and delicious desserts. It has not been in the country all that long however, and was introduced in the eighteenth century, first sold at a London market by a Mr Joseph Myatt in 1808. Most of the rhubarb grown in England comes from Yorkshire,

Rhubarb and Date Chutney

specifically from the 'Rhubarb Triangle' of Wakefield, Leeds and Bradford, and is recognised as a unique regional food! Not a combination which would immediately spring to mind - but try updating this true British classic with the addition of dates. This wonderfully saccharine, sticky fruit came originally from Iraq, and has been a staple food in the Middle East and the Indus Valley for thousands of years. They spread to Europe with the spice trade of the eighteenth century. The tartness of the rhubarb and the sweetness of the dates work perfectly together in this simple, yet elegant recipe.

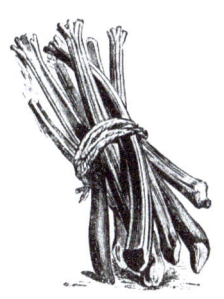

Rhubarb and Date Chutney

500g rhubarb

150g dates

250g red onions

200g apples (standard, eating apples)

250g soft, dark sugar

200ml wine vinegar

Spicing to taste (ginger, mustard and curry powder work well)

A pinch of salt

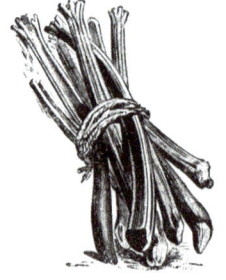

Rhubarb and Date Chutney

1. Finely slice the onions and cook them in a large, heavy-bottomed saucepan with the vinegar, allowing them to simmer for roughly ten minutes. **2.** Then, add the rest of the ingredients (spices included) - except the rhubarb. **3.** Slowly raise the temperature and bring to the boil. Then, lower again and simmer for a further ten minutes until the apples are nice and soft. **4.** At this point, add the rhubarb and cook for (roughly) twenty minutes - or until the chutney had gained a thick, 'jam-like' consistency. **5.** Take it off the heat, and allow to cool slightly. **6.** Place the warm chutney into warm, sterilised jars. Cover with a wax paper disc and seal. If you've got the patience, leave for a month before eating.

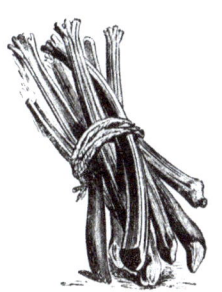

Roasted Lemon Chutney

"When life gives you lemons…
…. make chutney!"

This fascinating ingredient really deserves an entire section itself. Lemons have been used in British domestic kitchens for longer than you may think… The first substantial cultivation of lemons in Europe began in Genoa in the middle of the fifteenth century. The lemon was later introduced to the Americas and beyond in 1493 when Christopher Columbus brought them along on his voyages. It has been a revolution to the humble-home cook ever since! Not only an aid to general health and provider of vital vitamins, they are also helpful for digestion.

Roasted Lemon Chutney

Citrus fruits make wonderful-tasting tangy chutneys and pickles, and this one will have the most gorgeous, vibrant colour thanks to the lemon's natural hue. This recipe for spiced lemon chutney is a classic recipe to master; and will accompany such a wide variety of dishes; think middle eastern meats and couscous concoctions. This recipe uses both the juice and rinds - really making the most of this wonderful fruit.

Roasted Lemon Chutney

500g (unwaxed) Lemons
2 shallots
Spices (optional):

1 red chilli
1 clove of garlic
2cm piece of ginger (grated)
½ teaspoon coriander seeds
A pinch of salt
Olive oil (for roasting the lemons)

Roasted Lemon Chutney

1. Cut the lemons into roughly centimetre wide circles and remove the seeds. Place them on a baking tray with a small drizzle of olive oil and a little salt over the top. **2.** Finely chop the shallots, drizzle with the oil and a little salt and place on a separate baking tray. **3.** Roast both the lemons and the shallots - they will probably need about twenty minutes, or just until they start to brown. **4.** Once everything is cooked, place the lemons, shallots and spices (if you wish) in a large, heavy-bottomed sauce pan and mash with a fork. Although not quite How They Used To Do It, a food processor would speed up the process! **5.** Bring the mixture to a gentle simmer, and cook just for a few minutes to ensure all the flavours are combined. **6.** Place the warm chutney into warm, sterilised jars. Cover with a wax paper disc and seal. Leave for at least a week before opening.

PUMPKIN CHUTNEY

For something a little different....
....Why not try, 'Pumpkin Chutney'?

Pumpkin is a fantastically versatile vegetable as most parts of it are edible, including the fleshy shell, the seeds, leaves and even the flowers. In the middle east, pumpkins are used for sweet dishes, whilst it is commonly used as a savoury food in Europe. They are thought to have originated from North America though, where they were used by native americans in dried form - woven into mats.

Pumpkin Chutney

The name pumpkin originated from the Greek word for 'large melon' ('pepon') and this changed into the English version, 'pumpion' which Shakespeare referred to in his play, The Merry Wives of Windsor. This is a lovely autumnal chutney and the sweet, soft pumpkin goes very well with citrus as well as tomatoes or even other mixed fruits. Adding a little mixed spice or herbs will really add to this recipe. As a halloween side, you'll be sure to impress your guests with this!

Pumpkin Chutney

1 small pumpkin

1 large cooking apple

4 medium tomatoes

1 red onion

100g soft brown sugar

600ml cider vinegar

Spices:

1 red chilli

cumin, ginger, garlic, cardamom, turmeric, mustard seeds (optional, to taste)

1 orange or lemon (zested)

salt and pepper (to taste)

Pumpkin Chutney

1. Cut the pumpkin in half, remove the seeds and chop into small pieces. Chop the tomatoes and chop/core the apple. Slice the onion into thin pieces. **2.** Add all the ingredients, including the vinegar, sugar, any spices you desire and the zest of an orange or lemon, in a large-heavy-bottomed saucepan. **3.** Bring the temperature up to a boil, and then down again to a gentle simmer. Cook the mixture for about forty-five minutes, or until the pumpkin flesh is nice and tender. **4.** Take the saucepan off the heat and allow to cook slightly. If you are adding any fresh herbs, add them at this point to keep the flavours fresh. **5.** Pour the warm pumpkin chutney into warm, sterilised glass jars. Cover with a wax paper disc and seal. Leave for at least two weeks before opening, as this will allow the flavours to combine. **6.** Your chutney is ready to eat!

Pickled Pleasures

"HUNGER IS THE BEST PICKLE"

Benjamin Franklin (1706-1790)

Pickled Cucumber and Dill

PICKLED CUCUMBER AND DILL

Cucumbers are one of the most traditional ingredients for pickling, and when pickling began around 4000 years ago, cucumbers native to India were the first vegetables to be used! This dish was called 'achar' and has since become popular across the globe, spreading rapidly to western Europe, preserving precious seasonal vegetables throughout the year. The cucumber has long been used in Britain, and in the seventeenth century it was if anything, a little too popular! Samuel Pepys wrote in his diary on August 22nd 1663 that 'Mr Newburne is dead of eating cowcumbers.' Perhaps you can have too much of a good thing...

Pickled Cucumber and Dill

The dill in this recipe will work perfectly with the subtle cucumber, adding a distinctive taste with slightly bitter undertones. Try this delicious, tangy yet sweet pickle in ham and mustard sandwiches, alongside barbequed meats and as a complement to the classic piccalilli.

Pickled Cucumber and Dill

2 cucumbers
110ml white vinegar
80g caster sugar
1 ½ tablespoon salt
A sprig of fresh dill

Pickled Gherkins

The ultimate vegetable of the pickling world! Gherkins are actually a form of savoury pickled cucumber, favoured particularly in Britain and Australia. Like the pickled cucumber, gherkins are great in sandwiches, historically associated with Central Europe. Sometimes called a cornichon (the French word for gherkin), they have also been known as horned cucumbers, crumplings and guerkins. Try combining the traditional vinegar and dill flavourings with good sea salt, coriander seeds and garlic. This should provide a wonderfully crisp and fresh result, perfect with rich patés and cheeses.

Pickled Gherkins

1 kg gherkins (small cucumbers)

300g salt

700ml white vinegar

700ml water

2 cloves of garlic

2 sprigs of dill

2 tablespoons coriander seeds

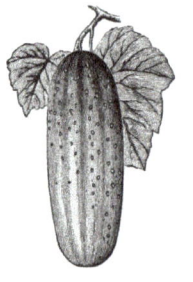

Pickled Gherkins

1. Ensure the gherkins are clean and presentable, then gently prick them with a fork. **2.** Place the gherkins, along with the salt into a large, ceramic or glass bowl and combine thoroughly. **3.** Leave this mixture to infuse for at least four hours. This process will result in a 'crisper' end pickle, as the salt dehydrates them. **4.** Once the gherkins have infused with the salt, wash them thoroughly in cold water. **5.** Take a large, heavy-bottomed sauce pan and add the vinegar, water, chopped garlic, dill and coriander. **6.** Cook very briefly on a low heat - to allow the flavours to combine. **7.** Add the gherkins to the vinegar solution (once it has cooled), and place in sterilised glass jars. Cover with a wax paper disc and seal.

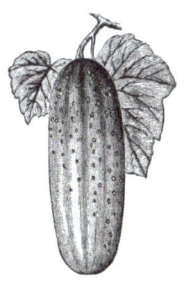

Lime Pickle

"Life - a spiritual pickle preserving the body from decay."

Ambrose Bierce (1842-1914)

This recipe really goes to show why home cooking is so rewarding. Lime pickle can be bought from many stores, and many people would be scared off making it, but this relatively simple pickle has such a long history, that it is a shame to see old skills go to waste. It was the saviour of many a sailor on a long voyage, preventing scurvy as well as preventing these precious fruits from going bad. The British Royal Navy particularly utilised lime pickle to great effect in warding

Lime Pickle

off scurvy on journeys to the new world. Consequently, it was around this time (about 1780) that chutney appeared as a popular appetizer dish in India. Lime pickle is a favourite accompaniment to Indian food, as the juicy, sour limes perfectly compliment the hot spices of a traditional curry. It can also be served with cold meats, or even better - homemade naan bread, pappadams and samosas to boot. So why not give it a go?

Lime Pickle

10 limes

Spices:

2 teaspoons mustard seeds

2 teaspoons ground cumin

2 teaspoons coriander

2 large garlic cloves

2cm piece of ginger

1 large red chilli

150g soft brown sugar

50ml vegetable oil

50ml water

50ml vinegar

2 tablespoons salt

Lime Pickle

1. Chop the limes into thick rounds and place them in a large ceramic or glass bowl with the salt. Mix the limes well, making sure that all the fruits are covered in salt. **2.** Leave the limes overnight to infuse. **3.** Heat the oil in a large, heavy-bottomed saucepan along with the spices. Cook on a medium heat for roughly one minute, until the aromas really come through. **4.** Tip in the lime mixture, water, vinegar and sugar and bring everything up to the boil. **5.** Then, lower the heat and simmer for at least fifteen minutes, until the mixture has achieved a nice, thick consistency. **6.** Take the saucepan off the heat and allow to cool slightly. **7.** Pour your warm pickle into warm, sterilised glass jars. Cover with a wax paper disc and seal. Leave the pickle for at least one week, to allow the flavours to really infuse.

PICKLED PEPPERS

Peter Piper picked a peck of pickled peppers.
A peck of pickled peppers Peter Piper picked.
If Peter Piper picked a peck of pickled peppers,
Where's the peck of pickled peppers Peter Piper picked?

If Peter Piper was able to pick his peck of pickled peppers - why shouldn't you!? Despite seeming exotic, peppers have been grown in Europe for some time, first appearing in Spain in the 1490s. Pickling these bright fruits was a fantastic way of preserving their colour as well as nutrients, and this dish has been a household favourite ever since.

Pickled Peppers

The misleading name 'pepper' was actually given by Christopher Columbus, upon discovering the plant and bringing it back to Europe. At that time, peppercorns were a highly prized condiment, and the name 'pepper' applied to any spices with a slightly hot and pungent taste. Hence the 'Pepper'! In this recipe, do feel free to mix the peppers with chillies, jalapenos, pimentos, different colours - red, green or orange, and sweet peppers too. Anything goes. Just make sure you keep track of where you're peck of pickled peppers is!

Pickled Peppers

500g peppers or chillies (a mixture is best!)

2 shallots

2 garlic cloves

450ml white wine vinegar

100g sugar

50ml water

A pinch of salt

Pickled Peppers

1. De-seed and de-stem your peppers and chillies, then slice them (as thick or as thin as you like) and pack them into a sterilised glass jar. **2.** Take a saucepan, and place the sugar, water, salt and vinegar in it. **3.** Bring everything up to a gentle boil, and stir until the sugar has completely dissolved. **4.** Then, pour the vinegar (whilst it is still hot) over the peppers / chillies. **5.** Cover with a wax paper disc and seal. Once cool, store your pickled peppers in the refrigerator, but leave at least twenty-four hours before eating them, to really allow the flavours to combine.

PICKLED FIGS IN BALSAMIC VINEGAR

For something a little different…
…. Why not try 'Pickled Figs in Balsamic Vinegar'?

Native to the Middle East and western Asia, the fig has been sought out and cultivated since ancient times, and is now widely grown throughout the temperate world. Figs were really common in Ancient Rome, and have since spread around the globe. Figs have only really been grown in Europe since the sixteenth century though, when Cardinal Reginald Pole introduced fig trees to Lambeth palace in London.

Pickled Figs in Balsamic Vinegar

Figs were a favourite of wartime Britain, and in the National Food Campaign Exhibition of 1940, they were among the fruits recommended for popular consumption! Mixed fruit puddings (containing figs) were especially well-liked, as well as the 'Fig Charlotte' which combined figs, sugar, brown bread and suet - all baked together in a pie-dish and served with custard. Scrumptious. Try this slightly unusual sweet pickle with roast meats, or utilise the fig-infused balsamic vinegar for a delicious salad dressing.

Pickled Figs in Balsamic Vinegar

500g figs
200g caster sugar
225ml balsamic vinegar
100ml water

Pickled Figs in Balsamic Vinegar

---

1. Take a large, heavy-bottomed saucepan and combine the sugar, vinegar and water. **2.** Cook over a medium heat until all the sugar has dissolved, and then add the figs (whole). **3.** Simmer for roughly ten minutes (or until the figs are just tender). **4.** Remove the saucepan from the heat and allow to cool slightly. **5.** Place the warm figs into warm, sterilised jars. Cover with a wax paper disc and seal. Your figs should keep for at least six months if properly sealed and refrigerated.

Revealing Relishes

"A MAN IS INSENSIBLE TO THE RELISH OF PROSPERITY 'TIL HE HAS TASTED ADVERSITY."

Saadi (1210-1292)

BEETROOT RELISH

Beetroot is a fantastic vegetable; a rich, velvety purple hue, earthy taste and silky smooth texture. It is also incredibly low in fat and packed full of vitamins, minerals and antioxidants. Luckily for us too, it is very easy to grow in the UK - a quintessentially English vegetable. Like many of the vegetables we have encountered in this book, it was first cultivated by the Romans but increased in popularity during the Victorian era. Its bright purple hue was used to liven up many a salad, as well as a sweet ingredient in desserts. With the advent of World War Two, food shortages and the increased need to preserve food, pickled beetroot in jars became the most widely available form of this foot stuff.

Beetroot Relish

With this in mind, why not hark back to the 'Blitz Spirit' and try this version of Beetroot relish for yourself?

As a final 'handy' hint, if your hands become stained whilst preparing the beetroot, just squeeze some lemon juice over them to help remove the purple colour.

Beetroot Relish

500g Beetroot

1 Onion

200g sugar

250ml white or red wine vinegar

2 teaspoons oil

Spices (to taste):

Mustard Seeds

Allspice

Cinnamon

1 Clove

Pinch of salt

Beetroot Relish

1. Peel and grate the beetroots. You should be looking for a small, rough - yet individual texture. **2.** Add the mustard seeds to a large heavy-bottomed saucepan on a medium heat. When they start to pop, add the onion (chopped), and then the sugar, oil, vinegar, salt, beetroot and the rest of the spices. **3.** Stir everything together to combine - and continue stirring over a medium heat. **4.** Once your mixture is combined, leave to cook for at least thirty minutes. The beetroot should be nice and soft. **5.** Add or remove liquid (water will do just fine), as the relish demands. **6.** Once your relish is cooked sufficiently, remove from the heat and allow to cool slightly. **7.** Place your warm relish into warm, sterilised glass jars. Cover with a wax paper disc and seal. Your relish is ready!

Chow Chow

CHOW CHOW

Had you heard of 'Chow Chow' before? It is a dish little known in Britain, but highly popular in the United States. It is a relish made from a combination of vegetables, mainly tomato, cabbage, onions, carrots, beans, asparagus, cauliflower and peas. It is traditionally associated with the Southern United States and soul food, as many claim it found its way to the South during the expulsion of the Acadian people from Nova Scotia. Still others cite a connection to the relish recipes of Chinese rail workers in the 1800s and Indian chutneys.

Now, its a great sweet topping for hot dogs and pinto beans. This complex history just goes to show how interlinked

Chow Chow

the culinary history of chutneys, pickles and relishes is… a mixture of immigration, emigration and regional tradition. The recipe you see here is actually inspired by one found in 'What Mrs. Fisher Knows about Old Southern Cooking', written in 1880. The vegetables are only a suggestion, so do feel free to use whatever you have around the house; afterall that's How They Used To Do It!

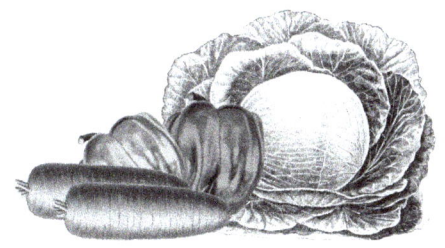

Chow Chow

1 small green cabbage

100g onions (chopped)

100g peppers (chopped)

100g cauliflower (chopped)

100g courgette (chopped)

100g carrots (chopped)

Spices:

2 tablespoons wholegrain mustard

1 teaspoon turmeric

1 teaspoon celery seeds

2cm ginger (grated)

400ml vinegar

300g sugar

Chow Chow

1. Combine all the vegetables, either chopped or finely sliced in a large, glass or ceramic bowl with a good sprinkling of salt. **2.** Leave the mixture to stand for at least six hours (or overnight). Then, wash the vegetables well under cold water. **3.** Place the vinegar, sugar and spices into a large, heavy-bottomed saucepan and cook over a medium heat until all the sugar has dissolved. **4.** Then, add all the vegetables and simmer for at least ten minutes. Quickly bring up to the boil, then take it off the heat. **5.** Allow the mixture to cool slightly, and then place the warm 'chow chow' into warm, sterilised glass jars. Cover with a wax paper disc and seal. As soon as it cools, it is ready to eat!

Corn Relish

CORN RELISH

"The discovery of a new dish confers more happiness on humanity than the discovery of a new star."

Jean Anthelme Brillat-Savarin (1755-1826)

Similar to 'Chow Chow', corn relish is a traditional recipe from the Southern United states. Despite this particularity, there is substantial overlap with American and European cooking, for example - did you know that a 'hamburger' is so called, because the German residents of Hamburg, who emigrated to America in the nineteenth century, brought over their traditional 'meat-patty' recipe? The American residents

Corn Relish

liked it so much, the name stuck! Corn relish travelled in the other direction though, as the vegetable was first grown in the Americas, and only travelled to Europe with the beginning of the trade network in the late fifteenth and early sixteenth centuries. Corn Relish was especially popular in the winter months, when fresh vegetables when in short supply. The bright colour and sweet taste never ceased to liven up simple, home cooked meals. Just like it used to do, corn relish will be great with your own hot dogs, burgers and salads. Enjoy!

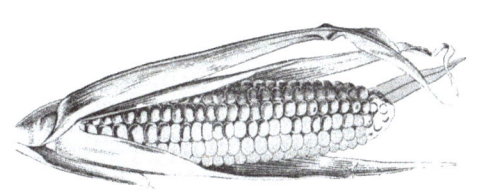

Corn Relish

500g fresh corn

1 white onion

150ml white wine vinegar

50g sugar

1-2 red chillies (according to taste)

1 tablespoon wholegrain mustard

1 small sprig of fresh coriander

A splash of olive oil

A pinch of salt

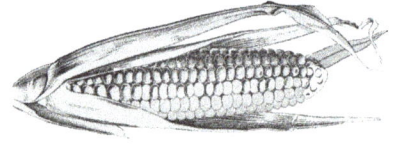

Corn Relish

1. Place the onion (finely chopped) with a little olive oil in a large, heavy-bottomed saucepan and cook until slightly translucent (about five minutes). **2.** Then, combine the rest of the ingredients; the corn, vinegar, salt, sugar, mustard and chillies (finely chopped). Leave out the fresh coriander at this point. **3.** Cook everything for roughly ten minutes, until the corn starts to gain a little bit of colour, and the sugar, herbs and vinegar have combined into a thin sauce. **4.** Once everything is sufficiently cooked, take the pan off the heat and allow to cool slightly. **5.** Add a handful of finely chopped coriander. **6.** Place your finished corn relish into warm, sterilised, glass jars. Cover with a wax paper disc and seal. Your relish is ready for eating!

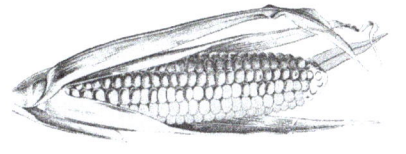

RED PEPPER AND WALNUT RELISH

Walnut relishes are very popular in France, but a relative rarity in England. This is a shame, because it really is a fantastic preserve which allows one to enjoy this nutrient-rich nut in a variety of ways. It is an ancient foodstuff which originated in Persia, but is now known as the 'English walnut.' The name derived from the Germanic wal- and the Old English wealhhnutu, literally meaning 'foreign nut.' It was obviously so popular, it had to be appropriated!

Red Pepper and Walnut Relish

Try if you can to retain the texture of the walnuts, by not making your relish too fine and avoid over-indulging on the sugar. Less is more in this recipe. The bright peppers will also add a bit of excitement and spice to the relish; and you can experiment with a couple of spicy / sweet red peppers too. It will be delicious with really simple dishes; meats, eggs and pulses - as its sweet earthy nature will allow the more subtle flavours to sing.

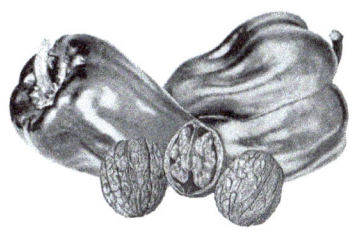

Red Pepper and Walnut Relish

100g walnuts

500g red peppers

100ml balsamic vinegar

50g sugar

1 clove garlic

1 tablespoon olive oil

1 teaspoon harissa or paprika

1 teaspoon lemon juice

A pinch of salt

Red Pepper and Walnut Relish

---

1. Lightly toast the walnuts in the oven, until they have slightly darkened in colour (this should take roughly ten minutes). **2.** Lightly roast the peppers, until they have softened sufficiently (this will probably take about twenty minutes). **3.** Once cool, coarsely chop the walnuts and seed, top and chop the peppers. **4.** Combine the peppers with the garlic, oil, salt, harissa, lemon juice and sugar - mix well, and then add the walnuts. **5.** Your simple relish is ready to be decanted! Just place the warm mixture into warm, sterilised jars. Cover with a wax paper disc and seal. It is best left for three days before serving, to allow the flavours to properly combine.

Gentleman's Relish

GENTLEMAN'S RELISH

For something a little different…
… Why not try 'Gentleman's Relish'?

"A gentleman is one who puts more into the world than he takes out."

George Bernard Shaw (1856-1950)

Gentleman's relish is a quintessentially English upper-middle class relish, mentioned in works of literature such as Nancy Mitford's novel The Pursuit of Love as a favourite food of the aristocratic 'Uncle Mathew.' In Angela Thirkell's Summer Half, the Gentleman's Relish sandwiches made for

Gentleman's Relish

adults attending a river picnic are instead wholly consumed by three adolescents, one of whom naughtily makes up a rude rhyme to 'Patum Peperium.' 'Patum Peperium' is the other, more refined name for this dish, which was created in 1828 by an Englishman called John Osborn. It is a type of anchovy paste with a strong, very salty and slightly fishy paste - containing butter, herbs and spices alongside the main ingredient. Today, the secret recipe is withheld from all but one employee at Elsenham Quality Foods in Elsenham, England; the licensed manufacturer. Gentleman's Relish is traditionally eaten thinly spread on slices of buttered white-bread toast, either on its own, or with cucumber or 'mustard and cress' sprouts. Although we'll never know the classic recipe, we feel this one may be just as good!

Gentleman's Relish

200g anchovies (a little goes a long way)
150g butter
2 tablespoons breadcrumbs
Just a pinch of:

cinnamon

nutmeg

cayenne pepper

ginger

black pepper

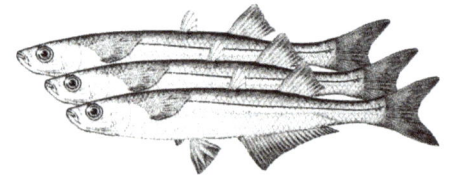

Cranberry and Orange Relish

The port adds a wonderful richness to what would otherwise be quite a zingy dish. As cranberries can be quite tart and sour, especially when under ripe, do feel free to add more sugar to according to taste.

Cranberry and Orange Relish

500g cranberries

1 orange (juiced and zested)

2cm piece of ginger

100g muscovado sugar

1 cinnamon stick

A good splash of port (optional!)

Cranberry and Orange Relish

1. Place the cranberries in a large, heavy-bottomed saucepan and cook them on a low heat until nice and soft. **2.** Peel the orange, and slice it very finely. Then juice it too, and add this peel and the juice to the cranberries, followed by the ginger (finely grated), sugar and the cinnamon stick. **3.** Cook everything on a medium heat for about five minutes to allow the flavours to combine. **4.** When the mixture has thickened slightly, pour in the port to loosen it up (here, water would work just as well). Stir in. **5.** Pour your orange and cranberry relish into warm, sterilised jars. Cover with a wax paper disc and seal. Your relish is ready to eat!

MEDITERRANEAN PICCALILLI

"So long as you have food in your mouth, you have solved all questions for the time being."

Franz Kafka (1883-1924)

In this section, celebrating 'sugar and spice' and 'all things nice' - what better time to experiment with a recipe turning traditional piccalilli on its head? Piccalilli is famed for the warm combination of spices; mustard, turmeric, ginger and garlic which give its its unique flavour. But this recipe uses hardly any spices at all! You can still achieve the delicious vegetable-mix of a piccalilli, but with the more subtle flavours

Mediterranean Piccalilli

of the mediterranean to provide a wonderful red colour, as opposed to the standard bright yellow condiment.

The mediterranean vegetables in this recipe make an unusual alternative as well as a delicious summer condiment; fantastic if you have a good supply of courgettes, peppers and tomatoes anyway. It can be served hot or cold.

Mediterranean Piccalilli

Vegetables to make up 1kg:
Aubergine
Courgette
Pepper
Onion
Tomato
A splash of olive oil
50g white flour
500ml white wine vinegar
100ml sugar
2 garlic cloves
Oregano, basil and rosemary (to taste)
A pinch of salt and pepper

Mediterranean Piccalilli

1. Chop all the vegetables into small chunks, and then add them with a little olive oil to a large, heavy-bottomed saucepan. **2.** Cook for five minutes on a medium heat, then add the garlic and continue cooking for a further ten minutes. Stir frequently. **3.** When the vegetables have begun to soften, take them off the heat. **4.** Combine the flour, herbs, salt and pepper in a bowl, with a splash of the vinegar. Stir this mixture until it forms a smooth paste. **5.** Pour the remaining vinegar onto the vegetables, alongside the sugar. **6.** Put the pan back on a low heat, also adding the spice and flour mixture - stirring constantly to avoid lumps forming. **7.** Cook until the sauce has slightly thickened then take off the heat and allow to cool slightly. **8.** Place your warm mediterranean piccalilli into warm, sterilised glass jars. Cover with a wax paper disc and seal. If you can resist, leave your piccalilli for at least two weeks before eating, to really allow the flavours to mature.

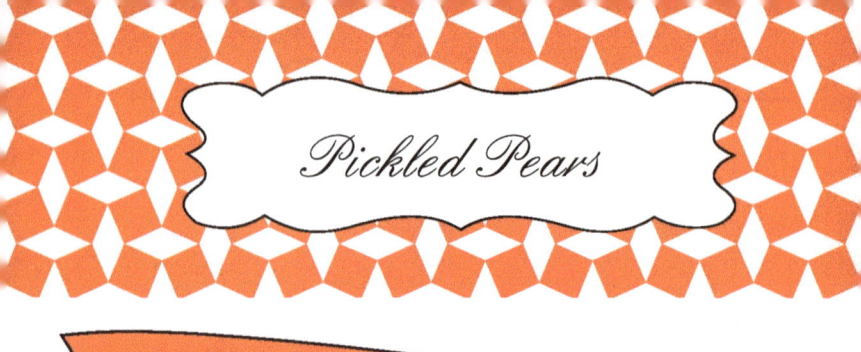

PICKLED PEARS

"A man watches his pear-tree day after day, impatient for the ripening of the fruit. Let him attempt to force the process, and he may spoil both fruit and tree. But let him patiently wait, and the ripe pear at length falls into his lap!"

Abraham lincoln (1809-1865)

This is a great introductory recipe to sweet pickles, as well as a stylish and sophisticated treat. The pears would make a lovely christmas present; with the whole spices left in the

Pickled Pears

jar, sealed and decorated with some pretty material. Try the pears with meringue or ice cream for a wonderfully decadent dessert. Pears are native to the temperate regions of Europe and are grown for their fruit as well as the beautiful pear blossoms. If you are lucky enough to have a pear tree in your garden, this is a fantastic way to use up a glut of seasonal produce. This recipe is actually inspired by a Roman cookbook, attributed to Apicius, called De Re Coquinaria, which had a set of directions for spiced, stewed pears.

Pickled Pears

---

1 kg pears

500g sugar

500ml white wine vinegar

3cm piece of ginger (sliced)

1 tablespoon black peppercorns

1 orange (juiced with the peel thinly sliced)

2 cinnamon sticks

5 cloves

Pickled Pears

1. Peel the orange, and thinly slice it. **2.** Combine the orange peel with the cloves, peppercorns, ginger, orange juice, vinegar, sugar and cinnamon sticks in a large, heavy-bottomed pan. **3.** Cook on a medium heat until the sugar has completely dissolved. **4.** Peel, core and halve (or chop) the pears. Add them to the rest of the ingredients and simmer lightly for about ten minutes. **5.** Once the pears are tender, remove them from the syrup and leave them to drain. **6.** Place the syrup back on the heat, and cook over a hot temperature until it starts to thicken, and has reduced to a desirable quantity (just enough to cover the pears). **7.** Then, place the pears into warmed, sterilised jars and pour over the syrup. Make sure to get an even amount of spices in each jar. **8.** Cover with a wax paper disc and seal. Your pickled pears are ready to eat - though are best left for at least three weeks to allow the flavours to mingle.

Sweet Chilli Chutney

SWEET CHILLI CHUTNEY

Chilli Chutney is a fantastic addition to the traditional English ploughmans with some mature cheddar, or great to give the humble sausage roll a modern twist! The Chili Pepper gets is spicy flavour from a substance called capsaicin, and vastly varies from the relatively mild cayenne pepper to the scorching habanero; known for its unique combination of intense flavour, aroma and heat. Chilli peppers were first domesticated around 6000 years ago in Mexico, and later spread to Asia and India with the advent of the spice trade and Christopher Columbus' explorations. Upon their introduction into Europe, chilis were grown as botanical curiosities in the gardens of Spanish and Portuguese monasteries. But monks experimented with the chili's

Sweet Chilli Chutney

culinary potential and discovered that their pungency offered a substitute for black peppercorns, which at the time were so costly that they were used as legal currency in some countries. They are relatively easy to grow at home though, even in the mild English climate, so why not give them a go? Feel free to make this recipe as spicy or as mild as you like, according to personal preference.

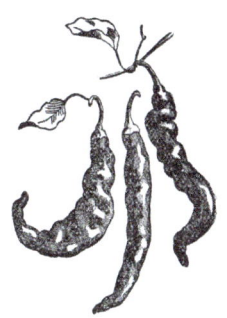

Sweet Chilli Chutney

500g tomatoes

200g apples

2 large red onions

2-3 red chillies (according to taste)

100g sugar

200ml white wine vinegar

1 tablespoon tomato purée

1 tablespoon paprika

1 tablespoon olive oil

Sweet Chilli Chutney

1. Place the onions (finely chopped) alongside a splash of oil in a large, heavy-bottomed saucepan. **2.** Cook them over a medium heat until slightly translucent (for about ten minutes). **3.** Then, add the tomatoes, apples, tomato puree, paprika and chilli. Cook for a further five minutes at least – or until everything has started to break down. **4.** Stir in the sugar and vinegar, making sure to stir regularly until the sugar has dissolved. **5.** Bring the heat down to a low simmer, and cook until it has achieved a thick, 'jam-like' consistency. **6.** Allow the mixture to cool slightly. Pour it into warm, sterilised glass jars. Cover with a wax paper disc and seal. Your chutney is ready to eat!

Grow your own...

"Unless the materials used are good you cannot expect perfect results. Discard all imperfect and overripe fruits, and the vegetables used should be up to standard. In spicing and pickling fruits and vegetables use only the best cider vinegar. If too strong it is better to weaken it with water than to buy weak vinegar which always lacks in flavour."

Mary M. Wright, Preserving and Pickling *(1917)*

Marrow Chutney

Marrow Chutney

This section celebrates the truly homemade aspect of this How They Used To Do It. Afterall, for many families in times of hardships, a small allotment with a few choice vegetables was the only option. These chutneys, pickles and relishes all utilise ingredients that are easily grown in the United Kingdom; cheap to produce and nutritious too. Vegetable marrow is a great place to start, as it is closely related to courgette, squash and pumpkin - all of which could be used in the same way in a chutney. Marrow will need a sunny position in well watered soil, preferably away from any cold, windy spots. It should be sown between april and june, and harvested between july and october. Good luck and happy growing!

Marrow Chutney

1kg marrow

200g onion

200g apples

2cm piece of ginger (sliced)

1 lemon
(juiced and zested - amount according to taste)

200g demerara or muscovado sugar

700ml vinegar

A good grind of black pepper

Marrow Chutney

1. Chop the marrow into small chunks and place in a large ceramic or glass bowl. Sprinkle it with salt, making sure everything is covered, and leave overnight. This will ensure your final chutney is nice and crisp. **2.** Once the marrow has been left for at least twelve hours, place it in a large heavy-bottomed saucepan along with the onions (chopped), apples (cored and chopped), ginger, lemon, pepper, sugar and vinegar. **3.** Bring everything up to the boil, and then reduce to a simmer. Cook while stirring constantly until the chutney has achieved a lovely thick, 'jam-like' consistency. **4.** Once sufficiently cooked, take the saucepan off the heat and allow to cool slightly. **5.** Place your warm chutney into warm sterilised glass jars. Cover with a wax paper disc and seal. Your chutney will keep for at least six months if stored in the refrigerator.

Pickled Nasturtiums

PICKLED NASTURTIUMS

*"Girls, do not scrub and cook and scour,
Until you have no time to plant a tree or vine or flower."*

Anon., Letters to Country Girls *(1853)*

Nasturtiums are wonderfully easy to grow annual flowers - whose leaves, seeds and flowers are all edible! Their vibrant appearance is the perfect for hanging baskets or plant pots around the front door, whilst their delicate fragrance also is lovely when cut, and placed around the house. Nasturtiums are rapid growers, so great for having fun with children too. They do best in full sun, and come in red, orange and yellow

Pickled Nasturtiums

variations - blooming in late summer and early autumn. Make sure to plant nasturtiums after the spring frosts in well-drained, sunny soil. These flowers can be grown in slightly shadier spots, but they do not bloom quite so well. Make sure to water regularly and prune the faded or dead flowers - as this will promote further blooming. Known as the 'poor man's capers', though a delicacy in their own right, try pickling nasturtium pods, which will appear as the flowers wither away. They have a distinct, mustardy flavour, wonderful with pâtés and cheeses.

Pickled Nasturtiums

200g nasturtium pods
(do adjust the recipe to as much or as little of these lovely pods as you can find)

60g salt

250ml water

200ml white wine vinegar

1 teaspoon sugar

1 bay leaf

1 sprig of thyme

Pickled Nasturtiums

---

1. Try to harvest the nasturtium pods while they are still young. As they mature, they will lose their crispness and flavour; so check for the bright green, still solid pods. **2.** Make sure to rinse the pods, to remove any dirt. Start by dissolving the sugar in the water to make a brine. **3.** Place the nasturtium pods in the brine, in a large jar - and leave for a couple of days. This should help the flavours to mellow slightly. **4.** After 1-2 days, strain the nasturtium seeds and rinse well in cold water to remove any excess salt. **5.** Place the vinegar and sugar in a large, heavy-bottomed saucepan and stir until the sugar has completely dissolved. At this point, add some finely chopped thyme leaves. **6.** Place the nasturtium seeds into the jam jars you are going to use, and pour over the still hot-vinegar and sugar solution. Add a bay-leaf too. **7.** Wait for the mixture to cool slightly, then cover with a wax paper disc and seal. Your nasturtium pods are ready to eat - though the flavours will mature with time.

Pickled Onions

PICKLED ONIONS

Onions are a really fun vegetable to grow at home; making a spectacular transformation from seed - to spindly grass, to round and ripe vegetable. They are also an incredibly versatile foodstuff, featured in so many recipes, both savoury and sweet. Sometimes, growing onions from seed can be a little tricky, but many people purchase baby onions in sets, and grow them on from this point. Onions only need a little water, but good, well-weeded soil is crucial.

A sunny spot also helps, and they are best grown in open ground, but could also be grown in short rows in deep containers or raised beds. Plant your onions outside in March or April, and harvest your well-earned vegetables from july to

Pickled Onions

september. This is a true classic of a recipe, a national treasure which is simple as well as delicious; pickled onions. Try with British classics such as fish and chips, ploughmans lunch or pork pies.

Pickled Onions

---

1 kg white, small onions
200g sugar (or double the amount of honey)

1 litre malt vinegar

20g salt

Spices:

Coriander, mustard seeds, black peppercorns and chili flakes (to taste)

Pickled Onions

1. Peel your onions (this will involve a lot of eye-watering, but placing a spoon in your mouth supposedly helps!) **2.** Sprinkle the salt generously over the onions, and leave overnight in a large, ceramic or glass bowl. This will help your onions stay nice and crisp in the final pickle. **3.** Place the sugar (or honey), spices and vinegar into a large, heavy-bottomed saucepan. Cook over a medium heat, stirring the sugar until it has completely dissolved. **4.** Pack the onions into the jam jars you wish to use, and pour over the still hot vinegar syrup. Make sure each jar has the same amount of pickling spices, and the liquid completely covers the onions. **5.** Cover with a wax paper disc and seal. Your pickled onions should be left for at least one month before consuming, as this will give the flavours time to mellow. Enjoy.

RADISH RELISH

"Preservation is a skill that has been known for many centuries, and as knowledge and methods improved, the housewife has been able to store a wider and wider range of the fruits of the earth upon her shelves."

National Federation of Women's Institutes,
Preserving, *1917*

Radishes are a very easy vegetable to grow; full of nutrients and great for the British climate. Their roots should be ready to harvest within four weeks of sowing them, again,

Radish Relish

fantastic if you are growing with children. For a continual supply of radishes, sow them roughly every two weeks throughout the summer - and even into the winter for the hardier varieties! Like onions, ensure that the soil in which your radishes are placed is well-weeded as well as watered. Their green tops are also edible and will make a delicious pesto when diced with parmesan, oil and pine-nuts. Perfect on a summer pasta dish. This relish has a wonderful pink tone, with a slightly spicy taste - it would make a great summer time accompaniment to barbecued meats.

Radish Relish

500g radishes (stemmed)
1 red onion
20g salt
200ml vinegar
200g sugar
1 tablespoon wholegrain mustard
1 tablespoon horseradish

Radish Relish

1. Finely chop (or slice) the radishes and onions. **2.** Leave the radishes and onions in a large, glass or ceramic bowl for at least a few hours, to ensure your end relish is nice and crisp. **3.** Strain the radish and onion, and wash thoroughly in cold water. **4.** Place everything in a large, heavy-bottomed saucepan (including the vinegar, sugar, mustard and horseradish). **5.** Bring it up to a gentle boil and cook for about fifteen minutes, or until everything is slightly softened. **6.** When sufficiently cooked, take the saucepan off the heat and allow to cool slightly. **7.** Pour your warm radish relish into warm, sterilised jars. Cover with a wax paper disc and seal. Your radish is ready to eat!

QUINCE CHUTNEY

For something a little different….
…. Why not try, 'Quince Chutney'?

"They dined on mince, and slices of quince, Which they ate with a runcible spoon; And hand in hand, on the edge of the sand, They danced by the light of the moon."

Edward Lear, The Owl and the Pussycat *(1871)*

Quince Charming: Quince are small fruits which belong to the same family as pears - and a much under-used and under-appreciated British fruit. Quince trees were first recorded in Britain in 1275, when Edward I planted four at the Tower of

Quince Chutney

London. They may have arrived earlier though, as thirteenth century English recipes included pie-crusts filled with whole quinces coated in honey and sprinkled with ginger. Gradually though, apples and pears edged them out of culinary favour - but now, the Quince is making a come back!

They are grown all over England, and are a treat to find. Pick them in October or November, leaving to ripen in a cool place if necessary. Quince trees are often propagated for their pretty pink flowers, but can also be used for a wonderfully light chutney. Quince has an earthy flavour, almost a cross between an apple and a pear, and is also commonly used as an accompaniment to cheese - so why not use it as an accompaniment a cheese course at your next dinner party?

Quince Chutney

500g quinces
500g apples
500ml vinegar
1 large red onion
400g muscovado or demerara sugar
Spices (optional, to taste):
ginger, cumin, mixed spice, cayenne pepper
A pinch of salt

Quince Chutney

1. Core, chop and peel the quinces and the apples. Slice the onion. **2.** Place the fruits and vegetables in a large saucepan, along with half the vinegar and cook over a medium heat. **3.** Cook the until the fruit is just soft. Then, add the sugar, spices and a pinch of salt. **4.** Simmer all the ingredients together until a thick, 'jam-like' consistency has been achieved. This should take roughly twenty minutes. **5.** Take the saucepan off the heat, and allow to cool slightly. **6.** Pour your warm quince chutney into warm, sterilised glass jars. Cover with a wax paper disc and seal. Voila, your chutney is ready to eat!

Growing Guide!

	Sow	Plant Out
Beetroot	March to July	
Cabbage	February to September	
Carrot	February to July	
Chilli	February to April	
Corn (sweetcorn)	April to May	
Cucumber	February to June	
Marrow	April to June	
Nasturtium	April to August	
Onion	Early March	Late March to April
Pumpkin	April to June	
Radish	March to September	
Rhubarb	September	October to March
Tomato	February to April	

Growing Guide!

Harvest	Good for?
June to October	Relishes or Chutneys
May to August, November to February	Relishes
May to October	Relishes or chutneys
July to September	Chutney
July to September	Relish
July to October	Pickles
July to October	Chutneys or Pickles
May to September	Pickles
July to September	Pickles
September to November	Chutneys
March to December	Relishes
April to July	Chutneys
August to October	Chutneys

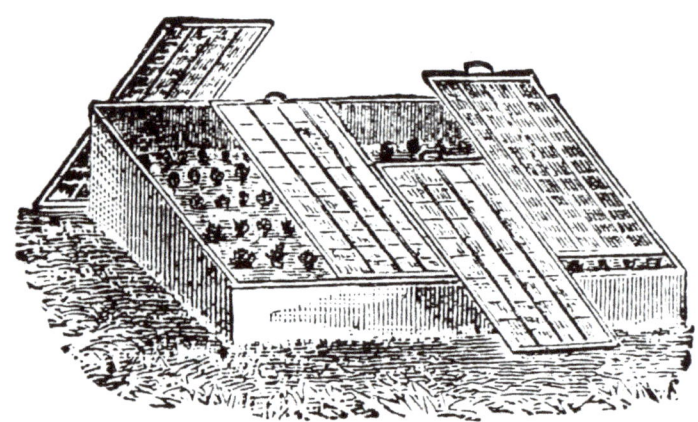

Serving Suggestions

Serving Suggestions

There are so many ways to serve pickles, chutneys and relishes, and hopefully we have given you some ideas with each recipe. The great thing about them, is that they can be paired with savoury or sweet foods alike - think quince or apple with cheese or rabbit, piccalilli with cold meats, cranberry with stuffing, date chutney with chocolate desserts or figs with ice cream. The list goes on. Try to think of the fruit, vegetable or flavouring on its own, and what foods you would pair that with normally – and then exactly the same will apply to your chutney, pickle or relish! For the beginners, try experimenting by using a new flavour in a tried and tested recipe. Half the fun is in the trialling, so be brave…

Serving Suggestions

HAVE YOU THOUGHT ABOUT?

Pepper and Walnut Relish with Curry?

Quince Chutney with Rabbit?

Gentleman's Relish with Scrambled Eggs?

Sauerkraut with Roast Meats?

Tomato Chutney with Savoury Salads?

Pickled Peppers with a Cassoulet?

Balsamic Figs with Ice-cream?

Pickled nasturtium pods with pâtés or blue cheeses?

Serving Suggestions

Gorgeous Gifts

Gorgeous Gifts

As we said in the introduction to this little book, the wonderful thing about making your own homemade products is the fun one can have with creating customised labels and garnishes to the finished jars (think finely chopped vegetables, citrus zest, herb sprigs). For the fruity chutneys, a few of the actual ingredients or even some of their flowers are beautiful accompaniments. Exactly the same applies for the vegetables, herbs and spices; whatever main ingredient you have used, save some back for decoration afterwards. Pickles, chutneys and relishes really do make the perfect vintage-inspired present as well as personal treat.

Make sure to source some lovely glass jars (kilner 'clip tops' work well, as do the traditional jam jar which you will find in

Gorgeous Gifts

most homeware stores). This will instantly make your creations look the part. As well as this, for serving chutneys or relishes at dinner parties, there are so many wonderfully decorated plates and bowls, so have a bit of fun! There are also antique sectional glass dishes, specifically made for serving an array of chutneys, pickles and relishes. At this point, you can make your own tags (think brown card and twine) to hang around the top of the jars, as well as handwritten labels to adorn the your containers. You could also place a little square of material ('gingham' is always lovely, though 'paisley' would also look a treat) over the top of your jar. Tied with some twine, this gives a great vintage-inspired twist to your presents, and we're sure the recipients will be touched by your efforts. Good luck, and happy decorating.

Ten Top Tricks and Tips

1. The vegetables should always be sound, preferably slightly under-ripe – clean and dry. Produce picked in wet (or even continuously foggy weather) makes chutneys and relishes which will develop mould in a very short time.

2. Use the natural seasons as your inspiration for ingredients - this is a great way to explore. Experiment with the recipes in this book, and just use what is growing, cheap and accessible near to you.

3. Always stir well (when cooking is required) to prevent sticking. A slightly undercooked chutney is preferable to one which tastes ever so slightly burnt.

4. Do not use too large quantities of fruit or vegetables at a time – large quantities are extremely difficult to handle without the proper equipment.

5. Whole spices are generally better than the ground spices, as they retain their strength longer. Use them whole if you can in pickles. If ground spice is used (for instance, in a chutney), freshly ground is best.

Ten Top Tricks and Tips

6. A pinch of bicarbonate of soda, added to very tart fruits (such as lemon or lime pickle) counteracts the acid, and less sugar is required.

7. Always have warm, sterilised jars ready for your chutneys, pickles and relishes. Sterilisation is really easy. The simplest way is to wash the jars in very hot soapy water, rinse in more very hot water, and place them into an oven on the lowest setting (275°F/130°C/Gas 1) for twenty minutes.

8. The type of vinegar you use is important: distilled white vinegar will not colour your ingredients, whilst cider vinegar gives a richer, slightly mellower flavour. Malt vinegar in turn, will provide a delicate, almost sweet taste.

9. Cover with cold spiced vinegar for a crisp pickle (red or white cabbage), use boiling vinegar for a soft pickle (beetroot).

10. Store in a cool, dry place. The greatest enemies to chutneys, pickles and relishes are mould and discoloration. As long as they do not encounter any steam or heat after production, and relatively little light, your products should keep for a very long time.

Credits and Attributions

Cover Image, Title page and Page 4 - This work is a derivative of "1956-Electrolux" is copyright © October 17, 2009 James Vaughn, x-ray delta one, made available on Flickr under Creative Commons Attribution 2.0 Generic (CC BY 2.0) http://www.flickr.com/photos/x-ray_delta_ one/4017899831/sizes/l/in/faves-90808113@N04/

Page 30 - This work is a derivative of "It's All You Need" is Copyright © 1950 Posted by noluck_ boston, made available on vintage-ads.livejournal.com http://vintage-ads.livejournal.com/tag/cleaning

Page 36 - This work is a derivative of "LIFE Dec 12, 1955 hamilton watches christmas spread" is Copyright © 1955, posted by Jocelmeow, made available on vintage-ads.livejournal.com http://vintage-ads.livejournal.com/tag/1945

Page 39 - This work is a derivative of "Maxwell House Coffee (1950) " is Copyright © 1950 posted by, pikkewyntjie made available on vintage-ads.livejournal.com http://vintage-ads.livejournal. com/tag/1950

Page 180 - This work is a derivative of "Tiffany Blue" is Copyright © May 18, 2008, Jill Clardy, made available on flickr under Creative commons Attribution 2.0 Generic (CC BY 2.0) http://www.flickr.com/photos/jillclardy/2523850043/

Page 181 - This work is a derivative of "UH-OH - Oreo / Nabisco, 1951" is Copyright © 1951, posted by Man Writing Slash (write_light), made available on vintage-ads.livejournal.com http://vintage-ads.livejournal.com/tag/1919

www.ingramcontent.com/pod-product-compliance
Lightning Source LLC
Chambersburg PA
CBHW061247230426
43662CB00021B/2451